VINTAGE HEARTS & FLOWERS

Vintage Hearts & Flowers

18 charming projects to make and give

KATE HAXELL

CICO BOOKS
LONDON NEW YORK

For my seven sisters: Anne-Marie, Clare, Gilly, Jinda,
Kelly, Nicky, and Victoria.

Published in 2008 by CICO Books
an imprint of Ryland Peters & Small
519 Broadway, 5th floor, New York, NY 10012

10 9 8 7 6 5 4 3 2 1

Text © Kate Haxell 2008
Design and photography © CICO Books 2008

A CIP catalog record for this book is available from the Library of Congress

ISBN-13: 978 1 906094 21 8
ISBN-10: 1 906094 21 7

Printed in China

Editor: Gillian Haslam
Designer: Roger Hammond at bluegumdesigners.com
Photographer: Debbie Patterson
Illustrator: Kate Simunek

Contents

Introduction

HEARTS AND FLOWERS, evocative symbols of romance and beauty, are combined here with the contemporary passion for vintage style to create 18 gorgeous projects you'll love to make and give.

Spending a happy day making something beautiful is every crafter's idea of pure bliss, and on these pages you will find days and days of crafting indulgence. From an embellished crazy patchwork heart to a woven paper card, a beaded lace flower to an appliquéd lavender heart, a knitted rose to an embossed metal token, there are projects here to suit a myriad of crafting skills. Each project is beautifully illustrated and clearly explained, so novices to a craft can proceed with confidence.

Most of the projects are sweetly small, so raid your scrap bag and button box for perfect pieces and spend happy hours in vintage shops discovering tiny treasures to incorporate into your own unique versions of these charming tokens of love and affection.

Kate Haxell

Knitted heart

An original twist on the traditional lavender sachet, these little hearts are quick
to knit and make charming gifts. You can make them in any yarn you wish, but use needles that
are a size smaller than recommended on the ball band to produce a firmer knitted fabric
that will prevent the lavender leaking out.

YOU WILL NEED

♥ *1¾oz ball of yarn of your choice*
♥ *Appropriate size knitting needles*
♥ *Knitter's sewing needle*
♥ *Two small pearl buttons*
♥ *Dried lavender*

OPPOSITE
This delicate pale
blue bobble heart is
knitted in a mohair
yarn for a beautifully
soft look.

HEART (MAKE 2)

Cast on 4 sts.
Row 1: Purl.
Row 2: K1, M1R, k2, M1L, k1.
Row 3: Purl.
Row 4: K2, M1R, knit to last 2 sts, M1L, k2.
Rep rows 3–4 seven times more. *(22 sts)*
Row 19 and following 8 alternate rows: Purl.
Row 20: K2, M1R, k7, MB, k2, MB, k7, M1L, k2.
Row 22: K2, M1R, k6, MB, k6, MB, k6, M1L, k2.
Row 24: K2, M1R, k5, MB, k10, MB, k5, M1L, k2.
Row 26: K2, M1R, knit to last 2 sts, M1L, k2.

Row 28: K2, M1R, k6, MB, k12, MB, k6, M1L, k2.
Row 30: K2, M1R, knit to last 2 sts, M1L, k2.
Row 32: K2, M1R, k9, MB, k10, MB, k9, M1L, k2.
Row 34: K14, MB, k6, MB, k14.
Row 36: K16, MB, k2, MB, k16.
Starting with a purl row, work 9 rows st st.
Next row: K18, turn.
Next row: P18.
Work on these 18 sts only.
***Next row:** K1, ssk, knit to last 3 sts, k2tog, k1.
Next row: Purl.
Next row: K1, ssk, knit to last 3 sts, k2tog, k1.
Next row: P1, p2tog, purl to last 3 sts, p2togtbl, p1.
Next row: Knit.
Next row: P1, p2tog, purl to last 3 sts, p2togtbl, p1.
Next row: K1, ssk, knit to last 3 sts, k2tog, k1.
Rep these last 2 rows once more. *(4 sts)*
Bind off.*
Rejoin yarn to remaining 18 sts.
Starting with a knit row, work 2 rows st st.
Rep from * to *.

abbreviations

k *knit*

k2tog *knit two together*

M1R *front to back, insert left-hand needle into strand between two stitches. Knit into back of strand*

M1L *back to front, insert left-hand needle into strand between two stitches. Knit into front of strand*

MB *make bobble. Knit into front and back of next stitch twice, turn, p4, turn, ssk, k2tog, pass first st over second st*

p *purl*

p2tog *purl two together*

p2togtbl *purl two together through the back loops*

rep *repeat*

ssk *one at a time, slip two stitches knitwise onto right-hand needle. Put left-hand needle through the stitches, in front of the right-hand needle, and knit the two stitches together*

st(s) *stitch(es)*

st st *stockinette stitch*

continued on next page

A delicate pearl
button provides the
perfect finishing
touch, echoing the
color of the yarn.

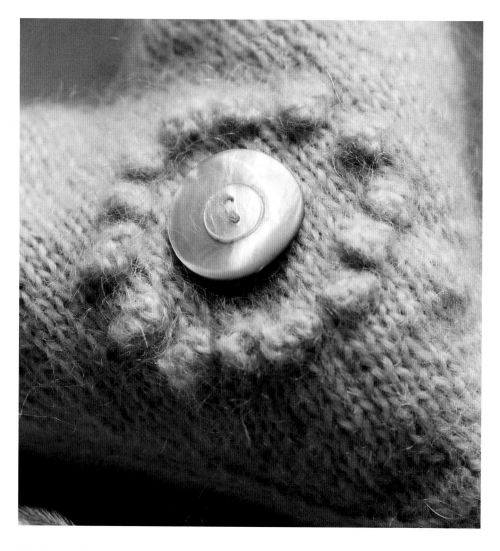

TO MAKE UP
Using the knitter's sewing needle and a length
of yarn, sew a button into the center of each
circle of bobbles. Using mattress stitch, sew
the two heart shapes together, leaving a small
gap. Fill heart with lavender (use a small
spoon to spoon the lavender through the
gap), then sew up the gap.

VARIATION

To knit a heart without bobbles, follow the pattern up to and including row 4. Then work as follows:

Rep rows 3–4 fourteen times more. (*36 sts*)

Starting with a purl row, work 13 rows st st.

Return to the main pattern and complete the heart by working from:

Next row: K18, turn.

You can incorporate any stripe repeat, a Fair Isle design or even a small intarsia motif into this heart pattern.

Pressed flower card

Bright, 1950s colors combine with checks and spots to make a pretty, retro-style greetings card that is sweet, but not overly sentimental. Once you have mastered the art of weaving strips of paper, this card is surprisingly quick to make.

YOU WILL NEED

- ✿ *Cutting mat, ruler, and craft knife*
- ✿ *Coordinating red and yellow spotted, checked, and plain papers, measuring at least 4³/₈in. in one direction*
- ✿ *Narrow- and medium-width double-sided tape*
- ✿ *5³/₄in. square, vanilla-colored greetings card blank*
- ✿ *Masking tape*
- ✿ *Scissors*
- ✿ *5³/₄-in. square piece of vanilla-colored thin cardboard*
- ✿ *24in. of ¹/₄-in. wide red and white gingham ribbon*
- ✿ *4 red and white vintage plastic buttons*
- ✿ *Yellow stranded embroidery floss*
- ✿ *Craft glue*
- ✿ *3 small pressed red flowers*
- ✿ *Sticky foam pad*
- ✿ *Butterfly motif*

I Using the ruler and craft knife and working on the cutting mat, cut strips of random widths from the spotted, checked, and plain papers. Place two strips of paper at right angles to each other, with the ends overlapping. Place two more strips next to the first ones, passing them underneath the strip previously overlapped, and vice versa, to start weaving the strips together.

2 Continue to weave the strips, passing alternate strips over and under to create a piece of woven paper measuring at least 4³/₈in. square.

3 Using the ruler and craft knife and working on the cutting mat, measure, mark, and cut out a 3¹/₄in. square aperture in the center front of the greetings card blank. On the inside of the card, stick strips of medium-width double-sided tape around the edge of the aperture.

continued on next page

OPPOSITE
Who would think that scraps of pretty papers left over from other projects could be turned into such a charming card?

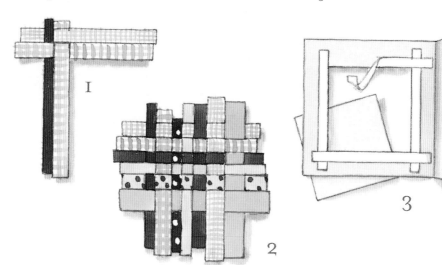

4 Peel the backing from the tape and lower the card onto the woven panel from the right side. Check that the panel is square within the aperture before you press the two surfaces together.

5 On the inside of the card, use scissors to trim off the woven ends to within 5/8in. of the outer edge of the card. Stick strips of masking tape around the edges of the woven panel to secure the ends of all the strips. Stick lengths of medium-width double-sided tape around the edges of the inside front of the card. Peel off the backing and stick the square of thin cardboard to the tape to cover the back of the woven panel.

6 Cut the gingham ribbon into four equal lengths. On the front of the card, stick lengths of narrow double-sided tape around the edges of the aperture. Peel off the backing, then press a length gingham ribbon onto the tape along each side, allowing the ends to overlap by approximately 3/4in. Trim the ends of the ribbon at an angle.

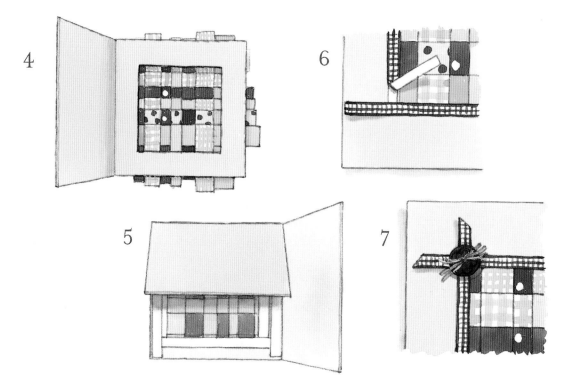

7 Thread stranded embroidery floss through the holes in each button and tie it in a knot on the front. Trim the ends to approximately ¹/₂in. long. Glue a button in place at each corner, where the ribbons overlap.

8 Glue three pressed flowers in random positions on the woven panel.

9 Use a foam pad to stick the butterfly to the left side of the woven panel. Bend the wings up a little to add further dimension.

8

9

VARIATION

This greetings card has a square of blue paper and a smaller one of checked scrapbooking paper glued to the front, with a woven panel of strips cut from a glossy magazine glued into the center of this background. A heart-shaped aperture is cut freehand into a small square of thin cardboard, which is then stuck over the woven panel using foam pads. Choose a boy-friendly color scheme and send this card to your sweetheart.

Ribbon flower

All you need is a long length of ribbon to make this stunning flower. It is so beautiful but so easy to make that you'll find yourself making whole bouquets. Use it as a corsage pinned to a lapel, to decorate a hairband, or attach one to a velvet ribbon and wear it as a choker.

YOU WILL NEED

✿ *24 in. of 1½-in. wide wired, double-sided taffeta, satin, or organza ribbon for each flower*
✿ *Sewing needle*
✿ *Sewing thread to match ribbon color*

I About ¾ in. from one end, fold the ribbon over itself at right-angles. Fold it over again, so that the long end is lying parallel to the short end.

2 Fold the long end of the ribbon over itself at right angles twice more to create a diamond shape. Keep folding in the same way until you have made 12 folds, so the diamond is three layers of folded ribbon thick.

3 Thread the end of the ribbon down through the hole in the middle of the folded ribbon diamond.

VARIATION

An organza ribbon flower makes the perfect topper for a beautifully wrapped gift.

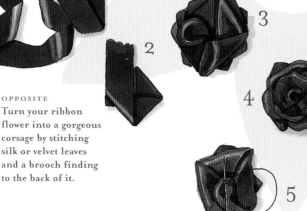

OPPOSITE
Turn your ribbon flower into a gorgeous corsage by stitching silk or velvet leaves and a brooch finding to the back of it.

4 Twist the end at the end at the back of the diamond clockwise. The top layer and then the second layer of folded ribbon will start to furl up, creating a flower. Twist until the flower is as tightly furled as you want it to look.

5 Thread the sewing needle. At the back, stitch back and forth through the edges of the ribbon in the middle of the flower to secure them firmly in position. Stitch the short end of ribbon (from Step 1) to the end protruding through from the front of the flower.

Appliqué lavender heart

Collect together small oddments of fabrics, vintage ribbons, and scraps of
delicate lace to make this pretty and sweet-smelling heart. It uses both machine- and
hand-appliqué and is a quick and engaging project to make.

YOU WILL NEED

♥ Heart template (see
   page 32)
♥ Patterned and plain
   cotton fabrics
♥ Fabric marker
♥ Scissors
♥ Fusible webbing
♥ Iron
♥ Sewing machine
♥ Sewing threads to
   match plain fabric,
   ribbon, and lace
♥ Ribbon and a lace motif
♥ Sewing needle
♥ Basting thread
♥ Dried lavender
♥ Linen button

I Enlarge the template to the desired size—
the heart shown here measures 7¹/₂in. from
V to point—plus ¹/₂in. all around for seams.
Using the fabric marker, draw around the
template onto the patterned fabric and cut
out the heart. Cut out another heart in plain
fabric and set it aside. Make another template
in the same shape, but 30 per cent smaller
than the first one, and draw around it onto
plain fabric. Using fusible webbing and an
iron, attach the small plain heart centrally to
the patterned one. Set the sewing machine to
satin stitch and, using matching thread,
appliqué the plain heart to the patterned one.

2 Baste the ribbon across the heart, about
4in. up from the base. Set the sewing
machine to a small straight stitch and, using

matching thread, stitch along each side of the
ribbon, as close to the edge as possible.
Remove the basting stitches.

3 Using the sewing needle and matching
thread, hand-appliqué the lace motif to the
center of the plain heart. Use tiny straight
stitches over the edge of the lace, making the
stitches as invisible as possible.

4 Embellish the heart further by stitching on
linen buttons. Right sides facing, lay the large
plain heart over the appliquéd one and follow
Step 8 of Crazy Quilted Heart (see page 39)
to make up the heart, using dried lavender as
the filling. In the V of the heart, stitch on a
bow made from a scrap of ribbon and finish
with a linen button.

LEFT
The central lace
motif on this heart
was cut from an old
doily, but you can buy
similar lace pieces in
notions stores.

ABOVE
If you wish, attach
a ribbon loop to the
V of the heart, so you
can hang the heart in
your closet.

Knitted rose

This is such a simple knitting pattern to follow and yet it makes a very effective full-blown rose. You can knit the flower in any type of yarn you have, using the size of knitting needles recommended on the ball band.

YOU WILL NEED

- ✿ Approximately ¼oz each of two colors of yarn of your choice
- ✿ Appropriate size knitting needles
- ✿ Scissors
- ✿ Knitter's sewing needle

getting it right

Use the following technique to make a perfectly gathered center for your flower. Having threaded the end of the yarn through the remaining stitches, tighten each one before pulling them all up. Using the tip of a knitter's sewing needle and working backward from the first stitch, pull each stitch tight in turn, then pull the end of the yarn through, taking up the excess from the last stitch.

OUTER PETALS

Using the thumb method, cast on 50 sts.
Starting with a knit row, work 5 rows st st.
Row 6: P4, twist, [p6, twist] rep to last 4 sts, p4.
Row 7: Knit.
Row 8: [P2tog] rep to end. *(25 sts)*
Row 9: Knit.
Row 10: [P2tog] rep to last st, p1. *(13 sts)*
Row 11: [K2tog] rep to last st, k1. *(7 sts)*
Break the yarn 6in. from last st.
Thread the end through remaining 7 sts and pull up tight.

INNER PETALS

Using the thumb method, cast on 44 sts.
Starting with a knit row, work 3 rows st st.
Row 4: P4, twist, [p6, twist] rep to last 4 sts, p4.
Row 5: [K2tog] rep to end. *(22 sts)*
Row 6: [P2tog] rep to end. *(11 sts)*

abbreviations

k *knit*
k2tog *knit two together*
p *purl*
p2tog *purl two together*
rep *repeat*
st(s) *stitch(es)*
st st *stockinette stitch*
twist *turn the point of the left-hand needle right around to the back, under the knitted fabric and back up to the working position, so putting a twist in the knitted fabric*

Row 7: [K2tog] rep to last st, k1. *(6 sts)*
Break yarn 6in. from last st.
Thread the end through remaining 6 sts and pull up tight (read the tip in the "Getting It Right" box for advice on gathering the center).

TO MAKE UP

Secure the gathered flower centers with a few stitches on the back. Using mattress stitch, sew up the flower seams. Place the inner flower on top of the outer one and stitch them together through the centers. Stitch a few loops of yarn into the middle of the inner flower to create the stamens. If you bring the needle up through the flower, then twist the yarn around tightly before taking the needle back down, the stamen will neatly coil around itself. You can then either sew the rose to your chosen garment or attach a brooch finding to the back.

OPPOSITE
This simple knitted rose can be used as a pretty embellishment for bags and clothes.

Sampler heart

This project is a wonderful opportunity for you to indulge your creativity and create your own unique heart sampler. It's not a big project, so the embroidery won't take long to do. A full stitch guide is given, but do substitute your own favourite stitches if you wish.

YOU WILL NEED
- ♥ Heart template
- ♥ 18-count evenweave linen
- ♥ Fabric marker
- ♥ 10½in. embroidery hoop
- ♥ Embroidery needle
- ♥ Stranded embroidery floss (use 2 strands throughout):
  One skein DMC 822 (A)
  One skein Anchor 376 (B)
  One skein Anchor 378 (C)
- ♥ Pins
- ♥ Sewing machine and sewing thread to match linen
- ♥ Toy stuffing
- ♥ Sewing needle and sewing thread to match embroidery floss C
- ♥ 28in. lightweight cord to match embroidery floss C

I Enlarge the template below to the desired size—the heart shown here measures 6in. from V to point—and cut out a paper template. Lay the template on the linen and draw around it with the fabric marker, then fix the linen into the embroidery hoop. Embroider the cross-stitch heart first, using color A and following the chart on page 25 and the photograph for position. Each cross-stitch is worked over two strands of linen.

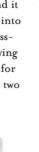

I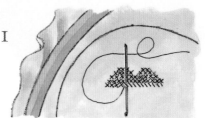

Enlarge this heart template to the desired size.

2 Then work the row of chevron stitch in color B, positioning it so that a straight stitch sits across the bottom of the heart. Work bands of embroidery stitches up towards the top of the heart, following the Sampler Stitch Guide on page 25 or using your own choice of stitches. Secure threads just outside the drawn line of the heart. When you get near the top of the heart, work the lazy daisies and French knots. Work more bands of stitches below the row of chevron stitch, working down towards the bottom of the heart, following the stitch guide if you wish.

continued on next page

2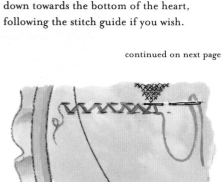

OPPOSITE
These cool colors give the sampler heart a Scandinavian feel, but it would also look beautiful worked in shades of pink floss on a cream linen.

3 Cut out the embroidered heart, cutting ⁵⁄₈in. outside the drawn line and being very careful not to cut any embroidery threads. Cut out another linen heart of the same size. Right sides facing, pin them together. Machine stitch around the heart, taking a ⁵⁄₈in. seam allowance and leaving a small gap for stuffing. Stuff the heart and slip-stitch the gap closed.

4 Using the sewing needle and thread, slip-stitch the cord around the edge of the heart, stitching it to the seam. At the top, form a loop of cord and stitch the ends together

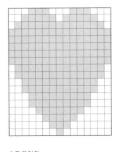

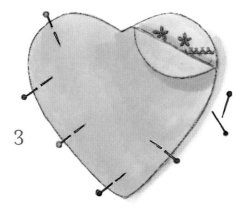

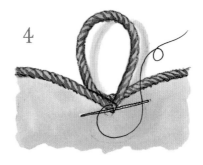

SAMPLER STITCH GUIDE
Bands of embroidery are 4 strands of linen apart. Letters A/B/C refer to the color of thread.

Top to bottom of heart:
Lazy daisy petals in C are over 6 strands.
Cross stitch heart in A (see chart above right).
French knots in A are over I strand.
Closed buttonhole stitch in B is over 3 strands high and wide.

Running stitch in C is over 2 strands.
Herringbone stitch in B is over 4 strands high and wide.
Chain stitch in A is over 4 strands.
Fly stitch in B is over 4 strands high and 8 strands wide.
Blanket stitch in C is over 3 strands high and wide.
Chevron stitch in B is over 4 strands high and wide.
Feather stitch in C is over 6 strands high and 3 strands wide.

Laced running stitch in A is over 3 strands.
Wheatear stitch in B is over 6 strands high and wide.
Open creatan stitch in C is over 8 strands high and 4 strands wide.
Double feather stitch in B is over 6 strands high and 3 strands wide.
Closed buttonhole stitch in C is over 4 strands high and wide.
Straight stitch stars in A have 7 arms over 5 strands and I arm over 9 strands.

Flower heart

Simple embroidery stitches and hand-appliqué give this asymmetric heart
a sweetly naïve style. The hanging loop is optional—you could sew a ribbon or a thin
cord or braid to the top of the heart and hang it from that if you prefer.

YOU WILL NEED

- ♥ *Asymmetric heart template (see page 28)*
- ♥ *Fabric marker*
- ♥ *Pink felt*
- ♥ *Flower template (see page 28)*
- ♥ *Pins*
- ♥ *Scraps of pale blue and pale brown felt*
- ♥ *Stranded embroidery floss (use 2 strands throughout):*
  One skein Anchor 921 (mid-blue)
  One skein Anchor 936 (mid-brown)
  One skein Anchor 970 (pale pink)
- ♥ *Sewing needle*
- ♥ *Toy stuffing*

OPPOSITE
**Felt is very easy to
work with as it does
not fray, but if you
want to use another
fabric, turn under a
narrow seam allowance
all around the heart
before working the
blanket stitch.**

I Enlarge the heart template to the desired
size—the heart shown here measures 4³/₄in.
from V to point. Cut two hearts from pink
felt (if using a printed fabric, make sure you
flip the template to draw the second heart so
that they are mirror images of each other).
Enlarge the flower template to two different
sizes appropriate to the size of the heart. Cut
five small flowers from pale blue felt and one
from pale brown felt. Cut one large flower
from pale brown felt.

2 Thread the sewing needle with a long
length of mid-blue embroidery floss.
Embroider different designs on each of

the pale blue flowers, using the photograph as
a guide. Embroider the small and large pale
brown flowers using mid-brown thread.

3 Arrange the large flower and pale blue
flowers on one pink heart, positioning them
at least ¹/₄in. in from the edges and using the
photograph as a guide. Pin them in place.
Using the appropriate colored embroidery
floss and short, straight stitches, appliqué the
flowers onto the heart.

continued on next page

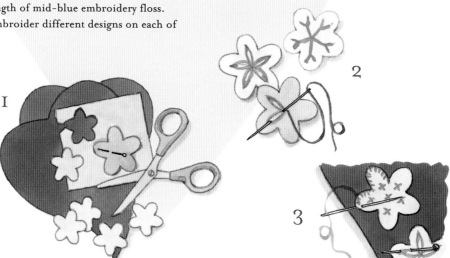

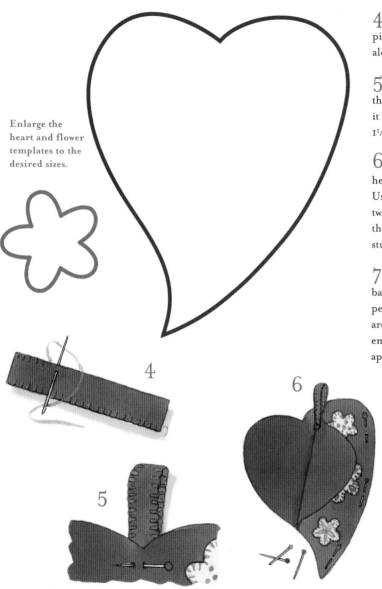

Enlarge the heart and flower templates to the desired sizes.

4 Cut a ¹/₂ x 4in. strip of pink felt. Using pink embroidery floss, work blanket stitch along both long edges.

5 Fold the strip of felt in half and pin it to the back of the appliquéd heart, positioning it centrally at the top to make a loop about 1¹/₂in. long.

6 Wrong sides facing, pin the plain pink heart to the back of the appliquéd heart. Using pink floss and blanket stitch, sew the two hearts together, trapping the loop into the stitching. Before completing the stitching, stuff the heart with toy stuffing.

7 Pin the small pale brown flower over the base of the loop, positioning it so that one petal is lying on the loop and the remainder are on the heart. Using mid-brown embroidery floss and short straight stitches, appliqué the flower to the heart and loop.

A smaller version of
the felt heart, decorated
with just a single flower
and strung onto a finding,
makes a pretty bag charm.
You could also use a
heart of a similar size
on a keyring.

Ring pillow

A romantic touch for a wedding day, this simple silk pillow will carry your wedding rings safely to the altar. Here it has been made and trimmed in ivory, but you could make one to complement your own wedding color scheme—perhaps using an offcut of the fabric used for bridesmaids' dresses, trimmed with the same lace.

YOU WILL NEED
♥ *Template (see page 32)*
♥ *Two 8-in. square pieces of silk fabric*
♥ *Fabric marker*
♥ *20in. of organza ribbon, 3/4in. wide*
♥ *Beading needle and beading thread*
♥ *Approximately 15 size-10 pearl beads*
♥ *24in. of organza ruffle trim*
♥ *Sewing needle and basting thread*
♥ *Two 1/4in. pearl disc beads*
♥ *Sewing machine and thread to match silk fabric*
♥ *Toy stuffing*

OPPOSITE
Tie your rings onto the pillow with a bow, then trim the ends to an angle. Don't make the bow too tight for nervous fingers to undo!

I Enlarge the template on page 32 to the desired size—the heart shown here measures 5in. from V to point—plus 1/2in. seam allowance all around. Draw around the template onto both pieces of fabric and cut them out. Fold the organza ribbon in half across its width and press with your fingers to make a crease. Open it out and pin the crease to the front of one heart, approximately 1 1/2in. down from and in line with the V. Using the beading needle and thread and size-10 pearls, sew the ribbon to the heart with beaded backstitch. Work the stitches in the usual way, but make them very tiny and pick up a bead for each stitch. Coil the ribbons up and pin them together to keep them out of the way for the next steps.

2 Starting at the V, baste the organza trimming to the front edges of one heart. The flat edge of the trim must align with the cut edge of the fabric, so the ruffles face inward.

continued on next page

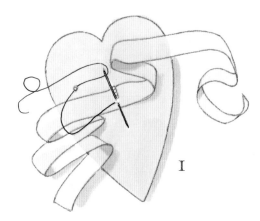

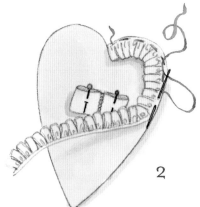

3 Lay the second silk heart face-down on the first one, sandwiching the trimming in between. Baste the hearts together around the edges, making sure that the ruffles remain lying flat and do not get caught in the stitches. Machine-stitch the hearts together taking a $^{1}/_{2}$in. seam allowance and leaving a 2in. gap. Remove the basting threads. Turn the hearts right-side out, stuff lightly and slip-stitch the gap closed.

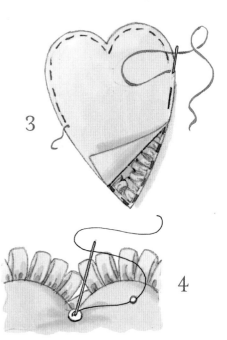

3

4 Embellish the V and the point of the heart with pearls. Bring the needle up through the pearl disc, thread on a pearl bead, then take the needle down through the disc to finish.

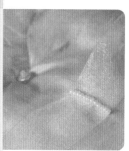

4

Enlarge the heart template to the desired size.

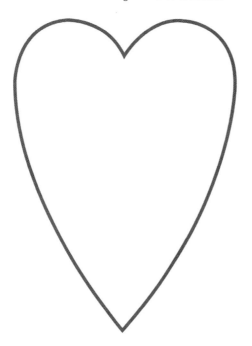

getting it right
Choose beads that complement your color scheme, or are used in your dress or those of your bridesmaids, to embellish your ring pillow. If your disc beads are colored, you can use tiny clear glass seed beads to attach them. If the beads are round rather than flat, sew them to the heart with tiny straight stitches (see Brooch Pillow on page 50).

Suffolk puff flowers

These puffs are often used in traditional quilting, but here they are turned into pretty, vintage-style fabric flowers. They are quick and easy to make and can be worn as a corsage, used to trim a summer hat, or to decorate a curtain tieback or the ends of a bolster pillow.

YOU WILL NEED
- *Pair of compasses and pencil*
- *Fabric*
- *Paper*
- *Scissors*
- *Iron*
- *Sewing thread to match fabric color*
- *Sewing needle*
- *Decorative button*
- *Bead*

I Using the compasses, draw a circle on the fabric twice the desired diameter of the finished flower and cut out. Cut a circle of paper 1/2in. smaller in diameter than the fabric circle to use as a pressing template. Place the paper template centrally on the fabric. Turning the edge of the fabric over the edge of the paper, press a narrow, even hem around the edge of the fabric circle. Remove the paper and turn the fabric over.

2 Using doubled matching sewing thread, stitch a line of small running stitches right around the fabric, stitching close to the pressed edge. Leave a long tail of thread at the start and end of the stitching.

continued on next page

ABOVE
A pearl button and bead make a pretty center for this lilac silk flower.

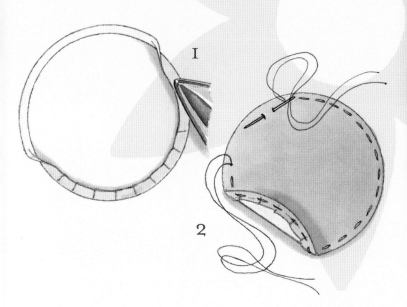

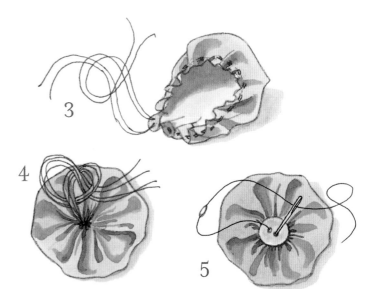

3 Pull firmly on both ends of the threads to pull up the gathers as tight as possible.

4 Tie the ends of the threads in a firm double knot and trim them short. Flatten the puff a little with your fingers, making sure that the gathered hole is in the middle.

5 Sew a decorative button into the center of the puff. Thread a bead onto the last stitch through the holes in the button for a final finishing touch. If you want to wear the flower as a corsage, sew a brooch finding to the back of it.

VARIATIONS

This flower is finished with two buttons placed one on top of the other, with two seed beads threaded on. Stitched to a gingham band, it makes a pretty curtain tieback.

A vintage button beautifully complements the antique lace fabric used for this Suffolk puff flower. This has also been used to decorate a lace curtain tieback.

Crazy quilted heart

Pick out favorite fabrics from your scrap bag to make your own unique version of this pretty heart. A limited color palette gives a sophisticated look and allows you to use lots of different embellishments without the overall effect becoming too crazy.

YOU WILL NEED
♥ *Heart template (see page 22)*
♥ *Pieces of silk and calico the size of the heart*
♥ *Fabric marker*
♥ *Scissors*
♥ *Pins*
♥ *Scraps of plain and patterned fabrics in chosen color palette (these should be cut to produce straight-edged irregular-shaped pieces)*
♥ *Sewing machine*
♥ *Sewing thread to match fabric color palette*
♥ *Embroidery needle*
♥ *Embroidery threads to match color palette*
♥ *Sewing and beading needles*
♥ *Beads, buttons, and scraps of ribbon and lace*
♥ *Toy stuffing*

I Enlarge the heart template to the desired size—the heart shown here measures 7in. from V to point—plus ½in. seam allowance all around. Cut out a paper template. Cut two hearts, one from calico and one from silk, and set the silk heart aside. Pin the first piece of patchwork fabric roughly in the middle of the calico heart.

2 Right-side down, lay a second piece of fabric over the first piece, ensuring that one edge is aligned with one edge of the first piece. Pin and machine-stitch along this edge, taking a narrow seam and stitching through all layers of fabric.

3 Fold the second piece of fabric right-side up and press the seam. At this stage do not trim the fabrics to match the calico heart.

continued on next page

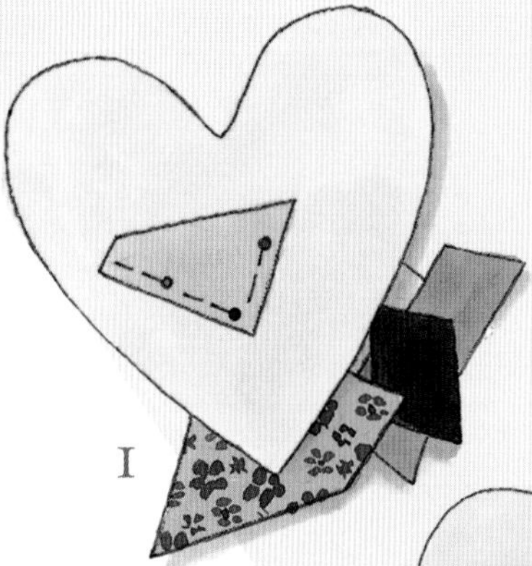

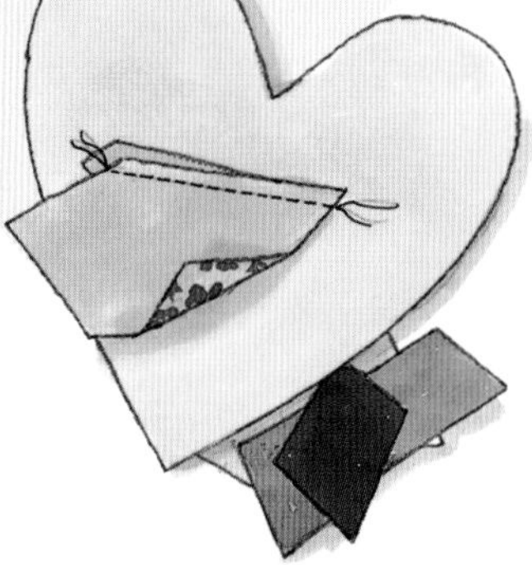

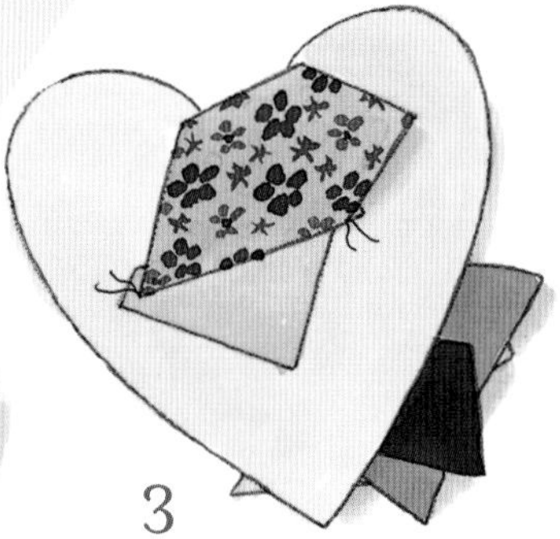

OPPOSITE
Beads of different types and tones and a selection of pearl and vintage plastic buttons decorate this gorgeous heart. A touch of blue makes a beautiful accent color in the pink palette.

4 Continue in this way, working around and out from the central piece. Make sure that each new piece of fabric aligns with a raw edge of another piece so that the only visible raw edges are outside the calico backing.

5 When all the calico is covered with patches, baste around the calico heart, ¹/₄in. in from the edge. Ensure that all the fabric patches are lying flat and smooth on the front. Trim off the excess patch fabrics around the edges of the calico.

6 Using a selection of different-colored embroidery floss and a variety of embroidery stitches, embroider over seams on the crazy patchwork. The stitches used on this heart are blanket stitch, chain stitch, feather stitch, fly stitch, and laced running stitch. Do not embroider any seams you want to embellish with ribbon.

7 Embellish the patchwork further using any techniques and materials you wish. Try sewing on beads (sew them to the fabrics and to the embroidery); adding simple embroidery to patches, such as lazy daisy flowers; or hand-sewing on pieces of ribbon and buttons.

getting it right

The secret to positioning the fabrics correctly is to take your time and be methodical. Lay each piece face down in position and pin it in place. Fold it right-side up and check that it is lying as you want it to. Remember that any not-so-perfect corners or slightly wobbly seams can be hidden with embroidery or other embellishments.

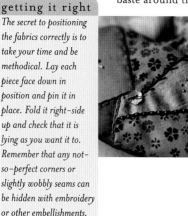

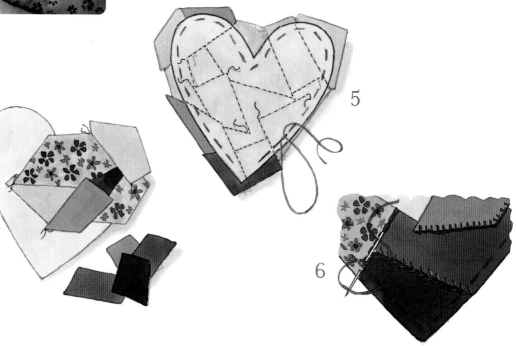

4

5

6

Sewing on buttons with embroidery floss and knotting and trimming the ends on the front of the button adds a pretty touch.

8 Right sides facing, lay the silk heart over the patchwork heart, aligning the edges. Machine-stitch all around, $^1/_2$in. in from the edge, leaving a small gap in one side. Clip the curves in the seam allowance, then turn the heart right-side out through the gap. Fill the heart with toy stuffing, then slip-stitch the gap closed.

7

8

VARIATION

This tiny version of the crazy quilted heart is decorated with a variety of embroidery stitches and has a ribbon loop for hanging.

Heart gift box

Give a special gift in this gorgeous pillow pack. Make it in colors
to coordinate with the present hidden inside for a perfect presentation that
will make a special occasion even more memorable.

YOU WILL NEED

- ♥ *Template (see page 43)*
- ♥ *Pale lilac, pale blue, and ivory thin cardboard*
- ♥ *Dressmakers' wheel*
- ♥ *Cutting mat, ruler, and craft knife*
- ♥ *Bone folder*
- ♥ *Scissors*
- ♥ *A section of lace-design vinyl tablecloth*
- ♥ *Low-tack spray adhesive*
- ♥ *Newspaper*
- ♥ *Lavender spray paint*
- ♥ *1in. circle punch*
- ♥ *Craft glue*
- ♥ *Pale blue mini brad*
- ♥ *Metal heart charm*
- ♥ *24in. of iridescent ribbon, ¹/8in. wide*
- ♥ *Iridescent glitter glue*
- ♥ *Narrow-width double-sided tape*

I Enlarge the template on page 43 to the desired size— the pack shown here is 5in. long. Transfer the template onto the pale lilac card by running the dressmakers' wheel over all the lines, embossing them onto the card. Using the ruler and craft knife and working on the cutting mat, cut out the shape around the outer lines. Using the ruler and bone folder (or the back of a table knife), score

carefully and smoothly along the inner lines. The side you have scored on will be the inside (wrong side) of the pack.

2 Using scissors, cut out small sections of the lace pattern from the tablecloth. Spray the back of the cut-out sections with low-tack adhesive, then press them into position on the right side of the card shape, as shown.

continued on next page

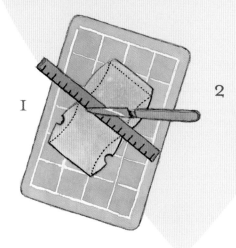

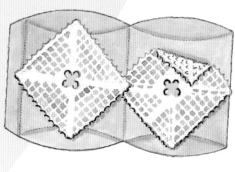

OPPOSITE
A hand-made gift box makes even the simplest present special, especially when the box is as pretty as this one.

3 Protect your work surface with newspaper and lay the cut-out shape flat on it. Working in a well-ventilated room, spray evenly over the card and lace with the lavender spray paint. Using the tip of the craft knife, carefully lift off the vinyl lace before the spray paint is completely dry, then leave to dry thoroughly.

4 Use the circle punch to punch small semi-circular sections opposite each other, as indicated on the template. These will provide a finger hole so that the inner flaps of the pack can be opened easily once it is assembled. Finger-press and fold along all the score lines to shape the pack.

5 Place the vinyl lace on a scrap of pale lilac card and spray over it with the lavender paint, as before. When dry, cut out a medium-sized heart with scissors: the hearts here were cut freehand, but you can use one of the templates in this book if you prefer. Cut out a larger heart from ivory card and a smaller one from pale blue card.

6 Glue the hearts together, layering them up as shown below. Using the tip of the craft knife, make a tiny slot in the center of the layered heart.

7 Push the brad through the metal heart charm, through the heart layers and finally

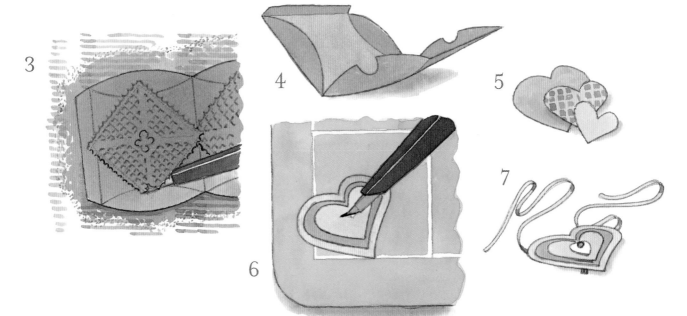

through the middle of the ribbon. Decorate the heart and the brad with iridescent glitter glue and allow to dry thoroughly.

8 Make a tiny slot in the center front of the pillow pack and push the arms of the brad through. Open out the arms on the inside to attach the motif to the pack.

9 Stick double-sided tape along the narrow flap of the pack. Peel off the backing, then stick the pack together along the straight edges. Tuck the ends in, punched edge first, to form the pillow shape. Tie the ribbon around the pack with the bow at one end, then trim the ends of the ribbon at an angle.

VARIATION

If you prefer, you can decorate your pillow pack with a stenciled flower motif and a flower charm. The petals of this flower are decorated with glitter glue and a purple brad holds the metal charm to the flower.

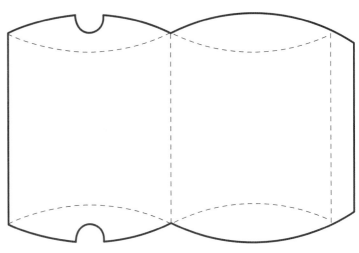

Enlarge this template to the desired size.

Quilted daisy pillow

If you are a quilting novice, or have found hand quilting difficult to master, then you'll love making this elegant pillow. The nature of chain stitch makes it far more forgiving of uneven stitches than traditional quilting stitch.

I Lay the batting on the cotton fabric, then the cream linen on top of the batting, carefully aligning all the edges. Pin and then baste the layers together, stitching ½in. in around the edges.

2 Sew lines of running stitches in both directions across the middle of the rectangle to hold all the layers in place while you quilt.

3 Enlarge the templates to the desired sizes and cut them out of paper—here, the larger daisy is 8in. across and the smaller one 6in. across. Arrange the templates on the linen and draw around them with the fabric marker. Draw around the outlines only, ignoring the inner circles.

continued on next page

OPPOSITE
Make your daisy pillow in linen and thread colors that perfectly complement your own interior color scheme for a beautifully coordinated look.

getting it right

Each time you need a new length of thread, trim the end to match the point in the color sequence with which you made the last stitch. In this way the color sequence will flow uninterrupted around the flower.

4 Thread the quilting needle with 36in. of variegated thread. Starting at the inner point of one petal, quilt around the drawn lines of both flowers using chain stitch. Make sure that each stitch goes through all the layers and pull the stitches taut.

5 When you come close to the end of the thread, make a holding stitch over the end of the last chain stitch, in the same way you would for a lazy daisy stitch. Secure the thread on the back. Bring the new thread up through the loop of the last chain stitch, and continue in the usual way. When you have finished the quilting, dampen the fabric to remove the drawn lines.

6 Thread the machine with brown sewing thread on the bobbin and the variegated quilting thread on the top spool: you may need to fit a size 90/14 needle to accommodate the quilting thread. On one long edge of a piece of brown linen, press under and machine stitch a ¹/₂in. double hem. On one long edge of the other piece of brown linen, press under a ¹/₂in., then I¹/₄in. hem and machine as before.

7 Thread the machine with brown sewing thread on the top spool. Work three buttonholes, spaced 3¹/₄in. apart, in the I¹/₄in. hem on one piece of linen.

8 Right sides facing, lay the piece of brown linen with the buttonholes on top of the piece of quilted cream linen, aligning the raw edges. Lay the other piece on top of this, also aligning the raw edges so that

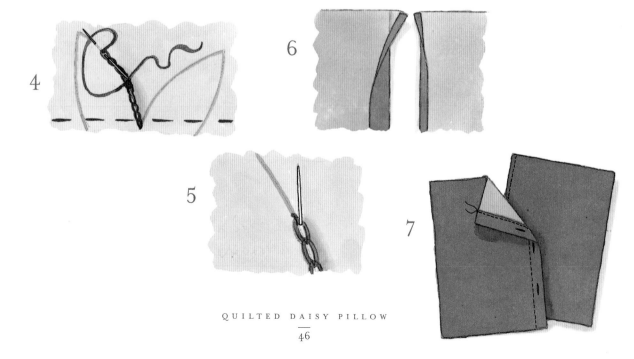

the hemmed edge overlaps the three buttonholes.

9 Pin and baste all the pieces together. Machine stitch around all edges, taking a 5/8in. seam allowance. Making the cover a little smaller than the pillow form ensures a well-filled pillow. Use the reverse function on the machine to stitch once back and forth over the overlap in the brown linen to strengthen it.

10 Clip the corners, remove all basting stitches, and turn the pillow cover right-side out. Sew on buttons to align with the buttonholes. Slip the pillow form into the cover and button it up.

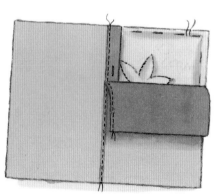

9

8

10

Enlarge this template to the desired size. Ignore the inner circle when stitching the flowers.

Knitted chrysanthemum

So simple to knit and so lovely to wear, this is an ideal project for a novice knitter—all you need to be able to do is cast on, knit, and bind off. Choose yarns to go with a favorite outfit and decorate the center of the flower with a personal charm.

YOU WILL NEED

✿ *Pair of US 2 (2.75 mm) knitting needles*
✿ *Small amount of Rowan Kidsilk Spray in Graphite (A)*
✿ *Small amount of Rowan Kidsilk Night in Oberon (B)*
✿ *Sewing needle and thread to match yarn B*
✿ *Charms*
✿ *Brooch back finding*

---

abbreviations

k *knit*
rep *repeat*
RS *right side*
st(s) *stitch(es)*

OPPOSITE

A pearl button, a diamanté gem, and a blue glass hanging gem decorate the center of this silver chrysanthemum.

Using A, cast on 4 sts.
Row 1 (RS): Knit.
Rep row 1 twice more.
*Row 4: K4, cast on 20 sts.
Row 5: K24.
Rep row 5 three times more.
Row 9: Bind off 20 sts, knit to end.*
Rep from * to * twice more.
Change to B.
**Row 22: K4, cast on 15 sts.
Row 23: K19.
Rep row 23 once more.
Row 25: Bind off 15 sts, knit to end.**
Rep from ** to ** eighteen times more.
Next row: K4, cast on 10 sts.
Next row: K14.
Rep last row once more.
Next row: Bind off 10 sts, knit to end.
Next row: K4, cast on 9 sts.
Next row: K13.
Rep last row once more.
Next row: Bind off 9 sts, knit to end.
Next row: K4, cast on 8 sts.

VARIATION

This flower follows the same pattern as the one shown in the main photo, but is worked in stockinette stitch, giving a very different look. Start with a knit row, then work the following and every alternate row in purl. The 1950s-inspired colors are complemented by a flat silver heart charm and yellow crystal bead stitched into the center.

Next row: K12.
Rep last row once more.
Next row: Bind off 8 sts, knit to end.
Next row: K4, cast on 7 sts.
Next row: K11.
Rep last row once more.
Next row: Bind off 7 sts, knit to end.
Next row: K4, cast on 6 sts.
Next row: K10.
Rep last row once more.
Next row: Bind off all sts.

TO MAKE UP

Starting with the bound-off end, coil the knitting around like a snail; make the first coil very tight then gradually enlarge the coils a little. Using the sewing needle and thread and working on the back of the chrysanthemum, sew the straight edges of the coils to the backs of the previous ones. Sew the charms into the front center and sew the brooch finding to the back center.

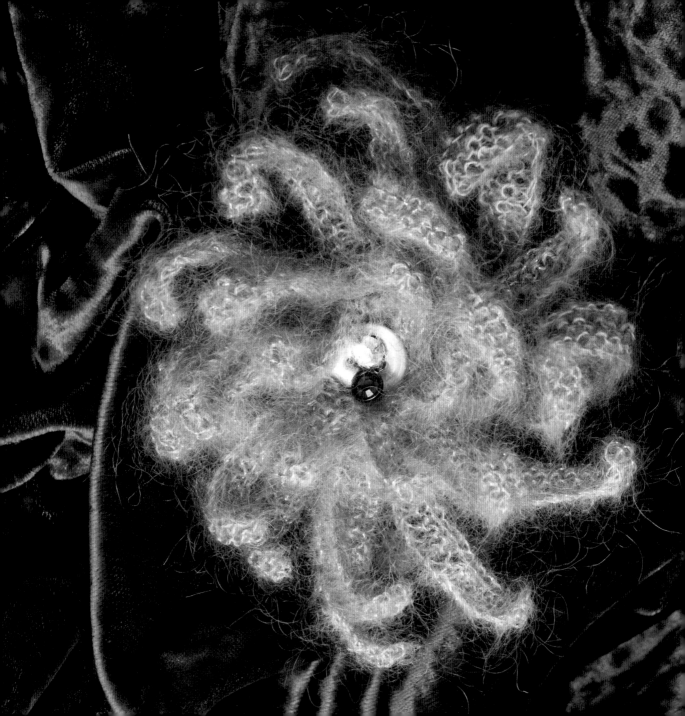

Beaded brooch pillow

With your most beautiful brooches pinned to it, this little heart pillow will add vintage glamour to your dressing table. Keep the bead embroidery simple, as too much will leave little space for your brooches. The beaded blanket stitch might look time-consuming, but it is easy to work and grows surprisingly quickly.

YOU WILL NEED
- ♥ Template (see page 53)
- ♥ Two 8-in. square pieces of velvet fabric
- ♥ Embroidery hoop
- ♥ Fading fabric marker
- ♥ Beading needle and thread to match fabric and ribbon
- ♥ Size-10 seed beads
- ♥ ¼in. cup sequins
- ♥ Size-7 seed beads
- ♥ Sewing needle and basting thread
- ♥ 20in. of taffeta ribbon, 1½in. wide
- ♥ Toy stuffing

I Enlarge the template to the desired size—the heart shown here measures 4⅜in. from V to point. Fix one square of fabric into the hoop and, using the fabric marker, draw around the template onto the fabric.

2 Thread the beading needle with a long length of thread. Working at least ½in. inside the drawn line and following the photograph, sew on size-10 seed beads to create two flower-like sprigs. Bring the needle up

through the fabric, thread on a bead, then take the needle back down close to where it came out. Repeat this to create all the lines of beads. If you wish, mark the lines with the fabric marker and sew on the beads following the lines.

3 At the start and end of every line of beads, place a sequin. Bring the needle up through the sequin, thread on a size-7 bead, then take the needle back down through the sequin.

continued on next page

OPPOSITE
Plump and pretty, this pillow will display your brooches perfectly, as well as keeping them to hand for when you want them.

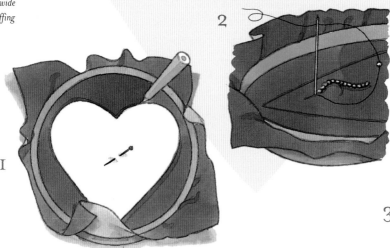

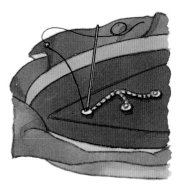

4 Take the fabric out of the hoop and cut out the heart, cutting ½in. outside the drawn line. With the fabric face-down to avoid crushing the pile of the velvet with the hot iron, press a ½in. hem all around. Avoid touching the sequins or beads with the iron as the sequins will shrivel up and the beads may break.

5 Fold under ¾in. at one end of the ribbon. Wrong sides facing, place the folded end in the bottom of the V at the top of the heart, aligning the edge of the ribbon with the edge of the heart. Pin the ribbon in place. Keeping the edges aligned, baste the ribbon to the pressed-under seam allowance all around; you may need to pull the seam allowance out a little to do this. When you reach the other end, fold under the end of the ribbon so that the fold butts up against the first folded end.

6 Using the beading needle and thread and starting at the V, work beaded blanket stitch all around the heart to sew the ribbon to the velvet. For each stitch, thread on a bead and push it down to sit against the fabric. Take the needle through the ribbon and velvet, as close to the edges as possible and a bead's width away from the last stitch. Loop the thread under the needle and pull the stitch tight, making sure the bead does not slip out of position.

7 When you have beaded all around the heart, secure the thread with a few firm stitches in the velvet seam allowance. Remove the basting stitches. Thread the beading needle with a long length of thread, double it and knot the ends together. From the back, bring the needle up though the velvet at the start of the line of beads. Take the

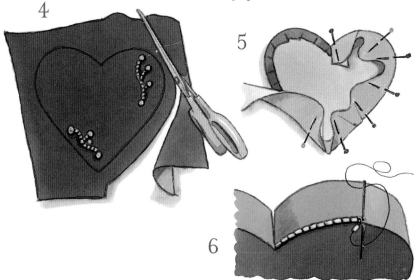

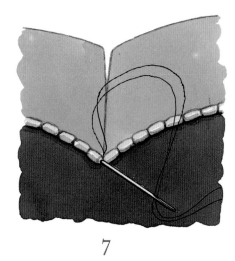

needle through all the beads and, when you reach the end, secure the thread with a few stitches in the seam allowance as before. The doubled thread will help to hold all the beads neatly in line. Do not pull the thread too tight or you will distort the shape of the heart.

8 From the other piece of velvet, cut out another heart of the same size and press under a seam allowance as before. Repeat Steps 5–7 to sew this heart to the other edge of the ribbon, carefully basting it in place so that it matches the first heart before beading around the edge.

9 Stuff the heart firmly through the gap between the two folded ends of ribbon. Finally, work beaded blanket stitch to close the gap.

VARIATION

This simpler version of the brooch pillow, without the ribbon gusset, will hold pins and needles in your sewing box. It is made from wool felt, decorated with a single swirl of translucent purple sequins and mauve delica beads, and beaded with the same mauve delicas.

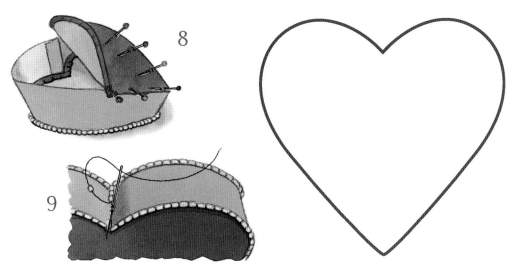

Enlarge this heart template to the desired size.

Hearts and flowers sampler

This pretty sampler combines heart and flower motifs in a design
reminiscent of traditional samplers, but with a fresh twist and clean colors
that fit perfectly into today's interpretation of vintage style.

YOU WILL NEED
♥ *8 x 8in. piece of 22-
   count evenweave linen
   in duck-egg blue*
♥ *Cross-stitch needle*
♥ *Stranded embroidery
   floss (use two strands
   throughout):
   one skein each of Anchor
   873, 871, 869, 845,
   843 and 842*
♥ *6in. embroidery hoop*

Fix the fabric into the hoop. Starting in the
middle of the fabric, stitch the dark-green
heart, working each cross-stitch over two
strands of fabric, following the chart. Next,

stitch the long "stem" of this heart to link the
flower to the large outer heart. Return to the
central flower and stitch out from the dark-
green heart to complete the design.

873
871
869
845
843
842

VARIATION

A simpler version of
the same design, worked
without the two smaller
hearts, is mounted within
a heart-shaped aperture in
a greetings card to send
to someone special.

OPPOSITE
Framed in a painted and
distressed pale wood,
the sampler makes a truly
pretty picture.

Bead lace flower

Based on a vintage Victorian lace motif found at an antiques fair, these flowers are created by machine-embroidering onto a film that can be dissolved away to leave just the embroidered lace flower. This is not a difficult technique to master, just remember that all the lines of stitching must join or the flower will fall apart.

YOU WILL NEED
- *Template (see page 47)*
- *Heavy-weight water-soluble film*
- *Embroidery hoop*
- *Ballpoint pen*
- *Sewing machine*
- *Sewing thread*
- *Small, sharp embroidery scissors*
- *Bowl of cold water*
- *Beading needle*
- *Size-10 seed beads*
- *½-in. wide satin ribbon*

I Enlarge the template to the desired size—the flower shown here measures 2in. across. Fit a piece of water-soluble film into the embroidery hoop and lay it over the template. Draw the flower onto the film using the ballpoint pen.

2 Thread the sewing machine, set it to small straight stitch and to free-motion embroidery. Lay the hoop under the needle so that the film is flat on the plate. Start by stitching twice around the outline of the

flower, ensuring that the second line of stitching is on top of the first line.

3 Stitch around the inner circle. Working in close concentric circles, fill the inner circle with stitches. Stitch back and forth across the circle in a spider-web pattern, joining the inner points of all the petals.

4 Keeping the machine running slowly but continuously, embroider each petal in turn. Stitch an elongated spiral within the petal.

continued on next page

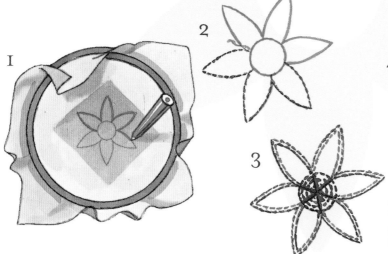

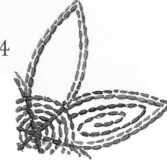

OPPOSITE
Cut the ribbon long enough to wrap around your wrist as a corsage, or to tie around your neck for a choker.

5 Then stitch up and down the petal, joining the tip to the inner circle. Stitch across the petal, joining the sides, then stitch from the middle down and across to the inner points of the petal. Work over each line of stitching twice. Move to the next petal by machining along the edge of the inner circle.

6 Take the film out of the hoop. Using embroidery scissors, cut out the flower, trimming as close to the stitching as possible without cutting it. Following the manufacturer's instructions, soak the flower in a bowl of cold water until the film has just dissolved (the residue will stiffen the flower). Arrange the petals on kitchen paper and leave to dry (see "Getting it Right").

7 Thread the beading needle with a long length of the sewing thread and secure to the back of the embroidery. Sew beads to the petals, weaving the needle in and out of the embroidery and threading on beads at random intervals. Cluster the beads more thickly in the inner circle.

8 Sew the flower to a length of satin ribbon, stitching through the back of the inner circle.

getting it right
If your flowers don't want to dry flat, pin them out starfish-fashion on an ironing board and leave them to dry like that.

5

6

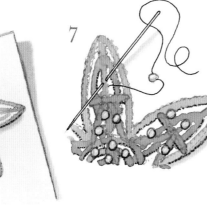

7

8

Metal heart token

This Scandinavian-style metal heart is so lovely no one will ever guess how quick
and easy it is to make. Try making several heart tokens to decorate your tree for Christmas,
but hang them out of reach of little fingers as the metal edges can be sharp.

YOU WILL NEED
- ♥ *Template (see page 61)*
- ♥ *Aluminum foil, 1/16in. thick*
- ♥ *Household scissors*
- ♥ *Masking tape*
- ♥ *Ball-point embossing tool or a dried-up ballpoint pen*
- ♥ *Hole punch*
- ♥ *Dressmakers' wheel*
- ♥ *Newspaper*
- ♥ *Green and brown antiquing wax*
- ♥ *12in. of pale blue satin ribbon, 1/8in. wide*

I Photocopy the template. Using scissors, cut
it out roughly and stick it to the aluminum
foil using masking tape. Draw over the design
using the embossing tool or ballpoint pen.
This side will be the back of the heart.

2 Using scissors, cut the heart shape out
around the edge of the template. Cut very
carefully, keeping the heart outline as
smooth as possible. Using the hole punch,
punch a hole for hanging, as indicated on
the template.

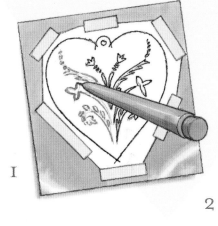

I

2

3 On the front, outline the heart using the dressmakers' wheel to create a row of evenly spaced dots around the edge.

4 Place the heart on newspaper and use your finger or a piece of kitchen paper to rub on first a little green, then a little brown antiquing wax. Leave to dry and buff following the manufacturer's instructions. Thread the ribbon through the punched hole, ready for hanging.

3

4

Enlarge the template to the desired size.

OPPOSITE
As well as decorating the house or tree for Christmas, this heart will make charming door decoration all year round.

VARIATION

You can make a greetings card to present the heart on. Cut a slot at the top of the card to thread the heart's ribbon through.

Flower buttons

Choose tiny scraps of silk and oddments of embroidery threads to make these sweet flower buttons. Three different flowers are shown here, but try combining other embroidery stitches to create your own flower garden of buttons.

YOU WILL NEED
❀ *Scraps of silk fabric*
❀ *4³⁄₈in. embroidery hoop*
❀ *⁷⁄₈in. self-cover button kit*
❀ *Fabric marker*
❀ *Stranded embroidery floss (use two strands throughout)*
❀ *Sewing needle*

I Place the fabric in the embroidery hoop. Lay the circle template that comes with the button kit on the back of the fabric and draw around it. Place the button back in the middle of the circle and draw around that as well. This smaller circle indicates the area in which to embroider.

2 Using two strands of embroidery thread and the sewing needle, and working on the front of the fabric, embroider a flower motif. Keep turning the hoop over to check that you are stitching within the inner marked circle. Follow the Flower Stitch Guide and the photograph to make the buttons shown here.

FLOWER STITCH GUIDE
Lavender: a line of backstitch in green with a row of French knots in mauve worked up each side.
Daisy: an eight-petaled lazy daisy in cream with a tiny mauve seed bead stitched into the center.
Snowdrops: French knots in cream with fly-stitch stems in green.

3 When complete, cut around the outer drawn circle. Assemble the buttons, following the instructions supplied with the kit.

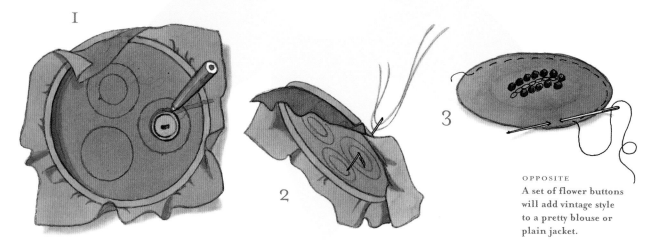

I

2

3

OPPOSITE
A set of flower buttons will add vintage style to a pretty blouse or plain jacket.

Acknowledgments
My thanks to the very talented
Sarah Beaman for making the
Pressed Flower Card, the Heart Gift
Box, and the Metal Heart Token.
Thanks to Cindy Richards at
Cico Books for suggesting
this book and Sally Powell for
keeping her creative eye on me;
to the lovely Gillian Haslam for
being the ideal editor and
Debbie Patterson for her evocative
photography. Kate Simunek
produced the beautiful and
informative illustrations, and
Roger Hammond brought
it all together perfectly on
the page.